TIGER,

Written by Marjorie Newman
Illustrated by Isabel Rayner

Collins Educational

An Imprint of HarperCollins*Publishers*

It's a Tiger's Life

Tigers live in the forests of China, Sumatra, Siberia, Indo-China, Pakistan and India. They are an endangered species and there are only between 4,000 and 6,000 still living in the wild. One hundred years ago there were 100,000.

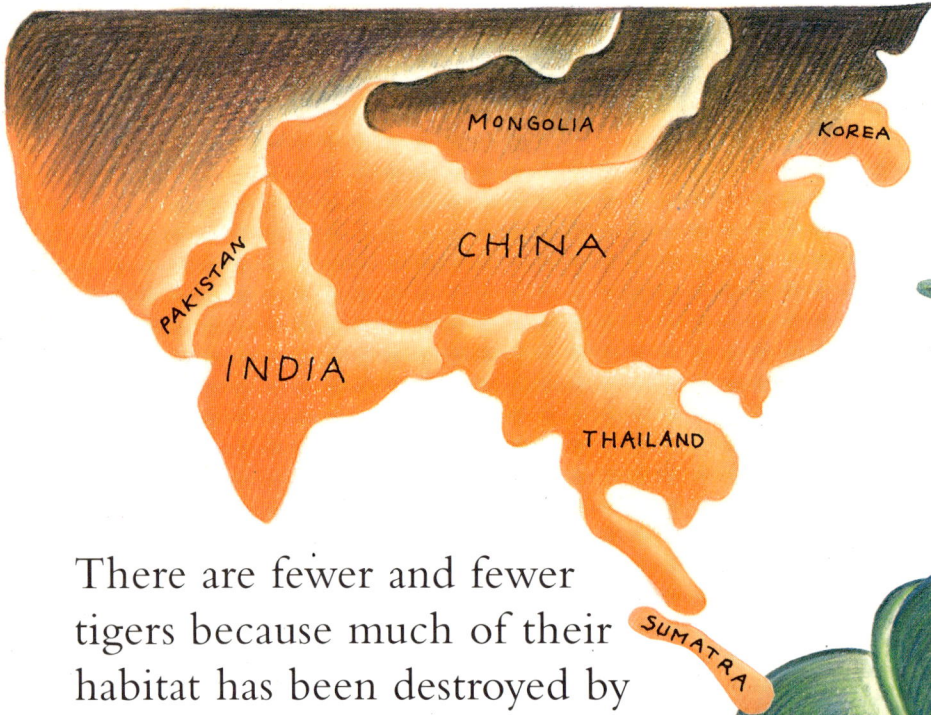

MONGOLIA

KOREA

CHINA

PAKISTAN

INDIA

THAILAND

SUMATRA

There are fewer and fewer tigers because much of their habitat has been destroyed by farming and by felling trees.

Tigers are hunted for their beautiful coats. Each has a different pattern of black stripes on an orange background. The stripes act as camouflage in the foliage, to hide the tiger. Tigers are also hunted for their bones which are sold as medicines.

Tigers are very strong and are able to run fast. They make good swimmers and often live near rivers. Tigers can also climb trees.

Tigers hunt animals like buffalo, bear and grouse for food and also catch fish to eat. They usually hunt at night and are very swift and silent. Since they can never be sure when they will next find food, tigers eat huge amounts when they can.

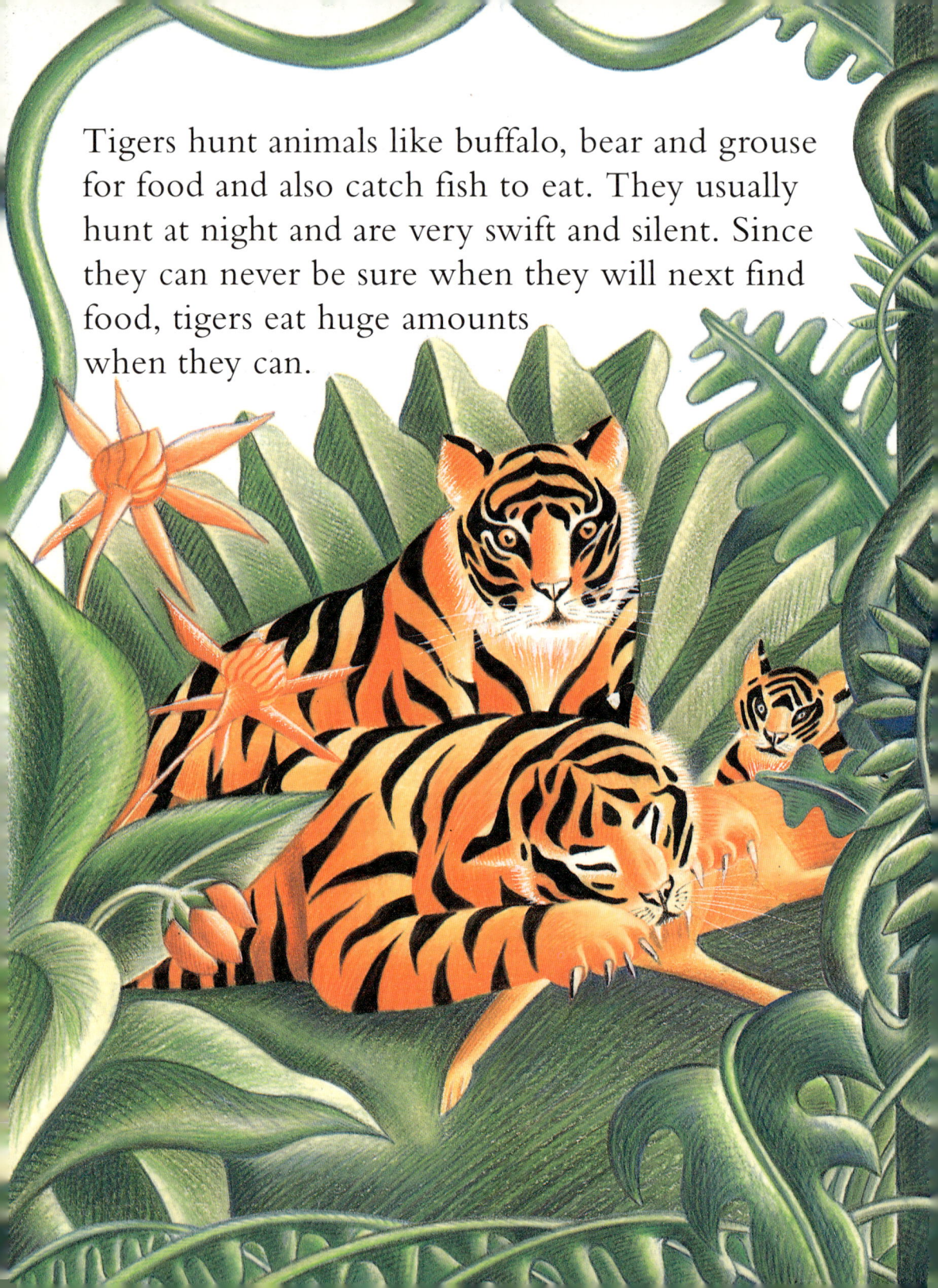

Tiger cubs are born blind but the tigresses feed and look after them. The cubs are weaned after about 100 days. They stay with the mother for about two years learning how to hunt and look after themselves. Then the young tigers go away to find homes of their own.

Tigers do not usually attack people. They like to live secretly and in peace.

The Five Little Foxes and the Tiger

A story from Pakistan – adapted by Marjorie Newman

Mr Fox was always boasting.
"I am very clever. No one
is cleverer than me!"

Then he would look at his wife,
and say, "Mrs Fox, you are not very clever.
You have only enough sense to fill one basket!"

Mrs Fox would smile at
their five baby cubs, and say nothing.

One day, Mr and Mrs Fox were out hunting for food. Suddenly they met a hungry tiger! "I am going to eat you!" the tiger growled. Mr Fox began to shiver and shake. But Mrs Fox kept calm.

She said, "How lucky we are to meet you, O great Tiger! Mr Fox and I need the help of the most important animal we meet."

The tiger was
very pleased to be
called important.
"What do you
want to ask?"
he said.

"Mr Fox and I have agreed to leave each
other," said Mrs Fox sadly.
Mr Fox looked at her in surprise.
Mrs Fox went on. "We cannot decide which
of us shall look after the cubs."
"If I'm to help you, I must see the cubs," said
the tiger craftily. He was very hungry.

8

This was what Mrs Fox hoped he would say.
"You will have to follow us home," she said.
Mr Fox could not believe his ears, but he was
too frightened to argue.
The tiger followed Mr and Mrs Fox to their
den, but he was too big to get inside.
"Wait here," Mrs Fox told him. "We shall have
to bring the cubs out to you."

Mr Fox was shocked.
The tiger waited outside.
Mr and Mrs Fox went into their den.

Quickly Mrs Fox hid the cubs as far from the entrance as she could. She whispered to them, "Keep very, very quiet."

"What are you doing?" asked Mr Fox.

"The tiger will get tired of waiting soon and he will go away," whispered Mrs Fox.

And the tiger did.

Now Mr Fox understood. Mrs Fox had saved all their lives.

After that, if anyone asked how clever he was, Mr Fox would answer, "Not nearly as clever as my wife!"

Mrs Fox would look at the cubs, and smile.

Tiger Jokes

If you threw a tiger
into the sea, what
would it become?
Wet.

What do tigers have that
no other animals have?
Baby tigers.

Why is a tiger like
a canary?
*Neither can ride
a bicycle.*

12

What is orange, striped and lives at the North Pole?
A lost tiger.

RAOR RAOR RAOR

NORTH

NORTH

NORTH POLE

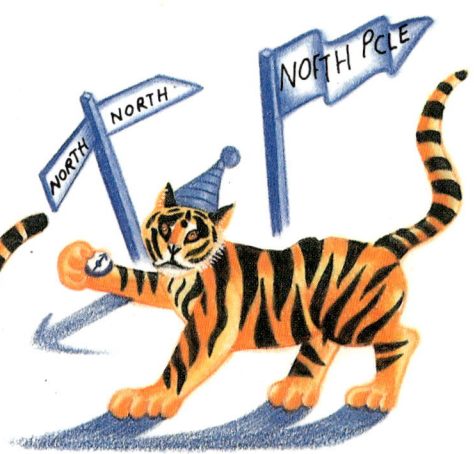

What is orange with black stripes and goes 'raor, raor'?
A tiger running backwards.

What's orange with black stripes and runs along the bottom of the sea?

A tiger in a submarine.

What's a tiger in a
fridge called?
Cold.

What's a tiger in a
small box called?
A tight squeeze.

Two tigers were walking in
opposite directions and met
on a track in the forest.
"Roar!" said the first tiger.
"Hee haw!" said the
second tiger.
"Roar?" said the first tiger, in surprise.
"Hee haw!" said the second tiger.
"What are you saying?" asked the first tiger. "Tigers
don't go 'Hee haw'!"
"But I'm new around here," said the second tiger.

Tiger and Anansi

A story from the West Indies – adapted by Marjorie Newman

A very long time ago, when all the animals lived in the forest, Tiger was King. The stories the animals told each other were called 'Tiger Stories'.

One day Anansi the spider said, "Tiger, many things have **your** name. Please can the stories be called 'Anansi Stories'?"
"Listen to little Anansi!" laughed the other animals. Tiger wanted the stories to keep his name.

He spoke craftily.
"If you can bring me a gourd full of live bees, and if you can capture Snake alive, then they can be Anansi stories."

He thought Anansi
would give up.
Anansi did not
give up. He walked
around miserably.

At last he spoke to Queen Bee.
"Tiger says I can't guess how many live bees will fit
inside a gourd! Will you help me?"
"You stupid spider!" buzzed Queen Bee,
flying away.

But by evening the bees felt sorry for Anansi.

"We will fly into the gourd one by one," they said. "Then you can count us."

The bees flew in while Anansi counted loudly. The moment the gourd was full he plugged the hole with a cork. He carried the gourd to Tiger.

The other animals were amazed.
Tiger pretended not to care. "You still have to capture Snake!" he said.

Tiger was sure Anansi could
never capture the huge snake.
But Anansi did not give up.

He laid a loop of rope on
the path, with bananas
inside the loop. When
Snake ate the bananas,
Anansi planned to
pull the rope tight.

Tiger and the other animals
watched and waited. Soon, Snake came along and
started to eat the bananas. Anansi pulled the rope but
Snake slithered safely away.

"Hard luck, Anansi!" laughed Tiger.

Anansi did not give up. He dug a hole, and made the sides slippery with grease. He put a pear at the bottom of the hole.
Then he waited.

Snake came along. She wrapped her tail around a thin tree and reached down and ate the pear. The she pulled herself out of the hole and slithered away.

Sadly Anansi set out to tell Tiger he had failed. On the way he saw Snake.

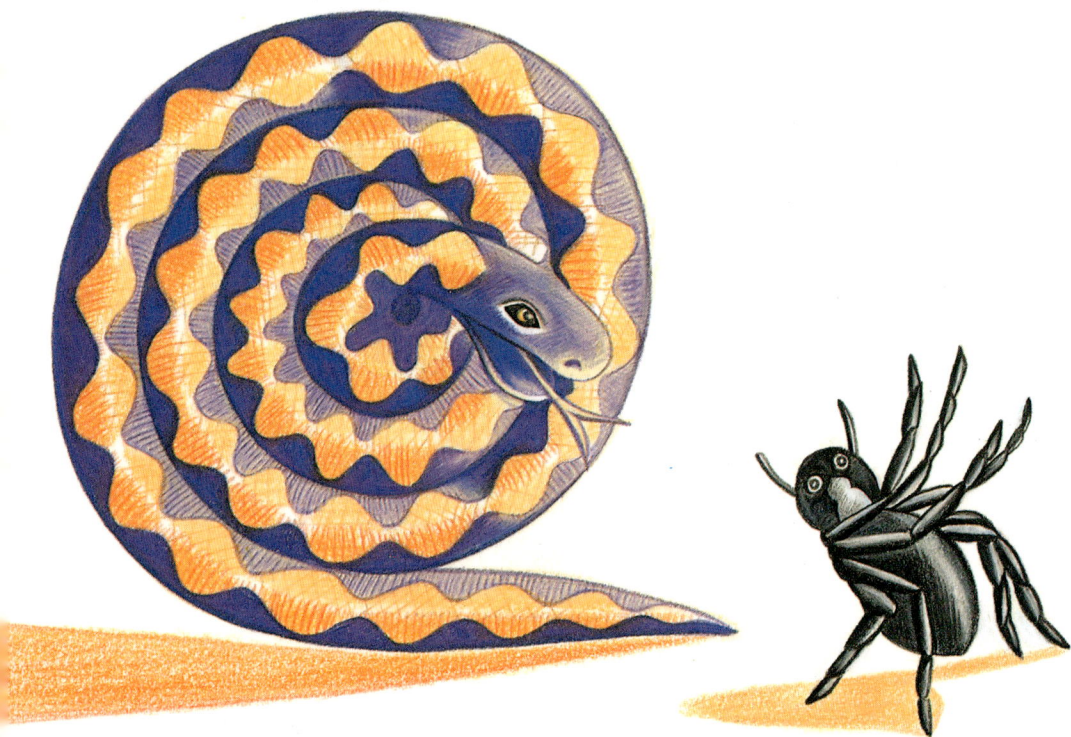

Snake was angry.

"Bird told me you are trying to catch me, Anansi! I think I'll eat you first!"

"No, No!" cried Anansi. He thought fast. "Tiger said you weren't as long as that bamboo tree. I said you were. I was only trying to measure you."

"I am the longest thing in the forest!" cried Snake. "Let's prove it!"

Quickly Anansi tied Snake's tail to one end of
the tree.
"Stretch out, Snake!" cried the other animals.
Quickly Anansi tied her middle to the tree.
"Stretch some more, Snake!"
cried the other animals.

Snake shut her eyes and
stretched with all
her might.

The moment Snake's head reached the top of the tree Anansi tied it firmly. Then he carried Snake to Tiger. Tiger was furious, but he kept his promise.

And from that day to this the stories are called 'Anansi stories'.

Tiger poems and rhymes

There was a young lady from Riga
Who rode, with a smile, on a tiger.
They came back from the ride
With the lady inside,
And the smile on the face of the tiger.

Anon

India

by W. J. Turner

They hunt, the velvet tigers in the jungle,
The spotted jungle full of shapeless patches –
Sometimes they're leaves, sometimes they're
hanging flowers,
Sometimes they're hot gold patches of the sun:
They hunt, the velvet tigers in the jungle!

The grass is flaming, and the trees are growing,
The very mud is gurgling in the pools,
Green toads are watching, crimson parrots flying.
Two pairs of eyes meet one another, glowing –
They hunt, the velvet tigers in the jungle.

The Greater Cats

by Vita Sackville-West

The greater cats with golden eyes
Stare out between the bars.
Deserts are there, and different skies,
And nights with different stars.

The Tiger

by *William Blake*

Tiger, tiger, burning bright
In the forests of the night,
What immortal hand or eye
Could frame thy fearful symmetry?

In what distant deeps or skies
Burnt the fire of thine eyes?
On what wings dare he aspire?
What the hand dare seize the fire?

And what shoulder, & what art,
Could twist the sinews of thy heart?
And when thy heart began to beat,
What dread hand? & what dread feet?

What the hammer? what the chain?
In what furnace was thy brain?
What the anvil? what dread grasp
Dare its deadly terrors clasp?

When the stars threw down their spears,
And water'd heaven with their tears,
Did he smile his work to see?
Did he who made the Lamb make thee?

Tiger, tiger, burning bright
In the forests of the night,
What immortal hand or eye
Could frame thy fearful symmetry?

Tiger and Hare

A story from China - adapted by Marjorie Newman

Hare was hopping through the forest when he saw some animals running away.

"What's wrong?" he asked.

"Mohan the Tiger is coming," they cried. "Mohan is King! He is big and strong!

If he is hungry he will catch you and eat you!"

The next moment,
Mohan the Tiger
walked into the clearing.
Hare did not run fast enough.
Mohan put out a great paw.
Thwack! Hare was caught.

Hare pretended not to be frightened.
"Good evening, Mohan," he said politely,
as he wriggled out from under Mohan's paw.
"Silence!" roared Mohan. "I am King of
the Forest!"

Hare thought fast.
"No. I am King of the Forest," he said.
"You! So small! So weak!" Mohan shook
with laughter.

"I will show you," said Hare. "Walk behind me along the path. Every animal is afraid of me, they know I am King. They will all run away when they see me coming."

Mohan thought about this. Could little Hare really be King of the Forest?

"Show me," said Mohan. "I will follow you.
If the animals do not run away, I shall know you are
not King. Then I shall eat you!"

Hare was frightened but led the way along the forest
path. Mohan the Tiger padded along behind him.

Sure enough, every animal ran away and hid.
Hare knew the animals were not running away from
him. Luckily Mohan did not realise it was him they
were running from!

"Hare!" Mohan said. "You are King of the Forest.
I will not trouble you again."
And he never did.